A Tree's Life

by Mateo Garza

illustrated by Louise A. Ellis

Characters: Squirrel, Nan, Ollie, Mom, Dad

Setting: A clearing in the woods

Squirrel: The Cash family has come to the woods for a picnic.

Nan: Dad, this is a good meal.

Ollie: I like this green apple.

Mom: We should go for a hike after this.

Dad: Yes, we can all go together.

(Later, the family returns from their hike and cleans up.)

Dad: That was a fun day!

Nan: That's the last of the trash.

Ollie: I hope we have a snack for the ride home.

Mom: We have some fruit.

Squirrel (eating the apple core): The family left this apple core. It makes a good snack.

(As Squirrel finishes the apple core, some seeds fall to the ground.)

4

(Squirrel is getting ready for winter.)

Squirrel: The apple seeds grew into a tree. The water from the rain will help it grow.

Squirrel: The Cash family is back. They are taking a walk and see a new tree growing. It will not have apples for a while.

Mom: Look, it's an apple tree.

Nan: I wonder if the apples will be red, yellow, or green.

(Squirrel is sleeping. The Cash family is playing in the snow.)

Ollie: Look! It's the apple tree!

Nan: It looks different without its leaves.

Squirrel (stretching): Spring is here! The apple tree is awake. It's much bigger now.

Ollie: Look at the pretty flowers.

Nan: The bees will help the apples grow.

Squirrel: Our tree began as a seed. Then it started to grow. The kids are older now. So is the tree.

Nan: Water, sun, and bees helped the apple tree grow.

Squirrel: The Cash family has come to the woods again.

Nan: I like eating outside.

Ollie: These are good cherries.

Mom: I wish we could come here all the time.

Dad: We will come back again.

Squirrel: The Cash family has cleaned up. But they left some cherry pits. Will a new cherry tree grow?

Respond to Reading

Retell

Use your own words to retell *A Tree's Life.* Tell what happens in order.

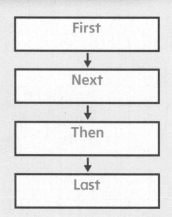

First

↓

Next

↓

Then

↓

Last

Text Evidence

1. Look at page 5. What happened after seeds fell to the ground?

   Sequence

2. Look at page 8. What happened when the tree got older? Sequence

3. How can you tell that *A Tree's Life* is a play? Genre

Compare Texts
Read about what's inside trees.

Inside TREES

Bark covers tree trunks. A new layer of bark grows each year. When a tree is cut, the layers look like rings. There is a ring for each year. Rings show a tree's age.

The lighter rings grow in spring and summer, and the darker rings grow in fall and winter.

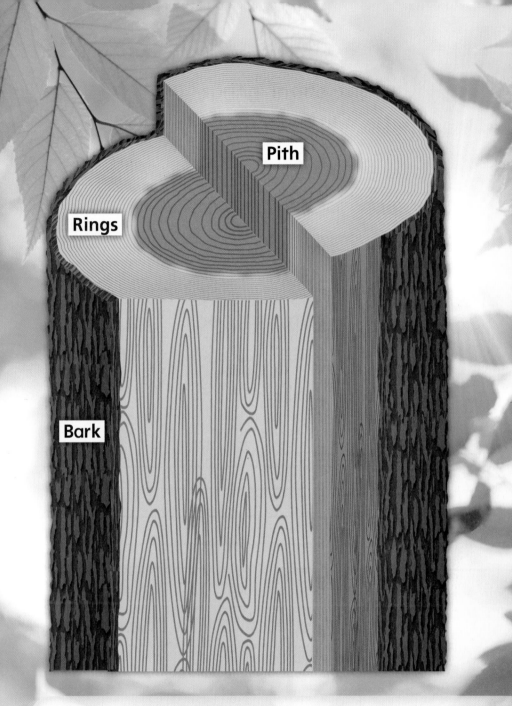

Pith

Rings

Bark

Make Connections
Which parts of the apple tree did you
see in *A Tree's Life*? Text to Text

Focus on
Science

Purpose To discuss which foods grow and which foods do not

What to Do

Step 1 Look at these foods.

strawberries crackers pancakes
bananas cucumbers muffins

Step 2 Make a chart like this one.

Grows	Does Not Grow

Step 3 Fill in the chart with the names of foods.

Conclusion Discuss your chart with a partner. Think of more foods that grow and foods that do not grow.